Our American Family™

I Am
Chinese
American

Amy Lee

The Rosen Publishing Group's
PowerKids Press™
New York

To Len—the best husband and research assistant an author ever had.

Published in 1997 by The Rosen Publishing Group, Inc.
29 East 21st Street, New York, NY 10010

First Edition

Book Design: Erin McKenna

Photo Credits: Cover © Nancy Ney/FPG International Corp.; photo illustration © Icon Comm./FPG International Corp.; p. 4 © Michael Krasowitz/FPG International Corp.; p. 7 © Peter Henschel/FPG International Corp.; p. 8 © FPG International Corp.; p. 11 © Bettmann; p. 12 © The Associated Press; p. 15 © Christian Michaels/FPG International Corp.; p. 16 © Su, Keren/FPG International Corp.; p. 19 © Peter A. Davis/FPG International Corp.; p. 20 © Ernest Manewal/FPG International Corp.

Lee, Amy.
   I am Chinese American / by Amy Lee.
       p.   cm. — (Our American Family)
   Includes index.
   Summary: Briefly discusses a Chinese American's heritage.
   ISBN 0-8239-5012-3
   1. Chinese Americans—Juvenile literature. [1. Chinese Americans.]
   I. Title. II. Series.
E184.C5T87 1997
973'.04951—dc21
                                        96-51076
                                          CIP
                                          AC

Manufactured in the United States of America

Contents

My Family

My name is Kimberly Chang, but my friends call me Kim. I live in San Francisco, California. My parents came here from a city called **Beijing** (bay-ZHING), in the country of China. I have a big brother named Chao. His American name is Charles. My parents teach my brother and me about the rich **culture** (KUL-cher) of China.

My parents own a bakery. They work there together. My brother helps them after school. When I am older, I will help out too.

◀ You learn about American history at school. But you can also learn about your heritage from your family.

5

Beijing

Beijing is the capital of China. In Beijing, my parents lived in a small apartment with my grandparents. In the evenings, they liked to visit with other families in the building.

Everyone in the family got up early to start their day. My father worked in a factory. My mother worked in a library. In China, most people work six days a week. My parents worked six days a week too. But on their day off, they often went to the park and had a picnic.

Beijing is full of historical places. One of these places is the Imperial Palace. ▶

Confucius

My family follows the teachings of a man named **Confucius** (kun-FYOO-shus). Confucius was a Chinese **sage** (SAYJ) who lived about 2,500 years ago. Confucius believed that people should respect each other and work together for the good of everyone. He taught many Chinese people how to live in peace and friendship. Many listened to him. Today, people around the world still follow the teachings of Confucius.

◀ The words of Confucius were recorded in a book called the *Analects*. People still read it today.

Chinese New Year

The Chinese New Year is an important Chinese holiday. It happens at the end of January or in early February. There is a big parade in an area of San Francisco called Chinatown. My brother and I like to watch it together. Bells and firecrackers are used in the parade to scare away evil spirits. At home, we celebrate the New Year with a special meal. Our house is decorated in red, which stands for good luck. Children get money in red envelopes. We all have fun.

The huge paper dragon used in the parade is meant to bring good luck in the New Year. A long line of people ▶ walk underneath it to hold it up.

A Famous Chinese American

Yo-Yo Ma is someone I admire very much. He grew up around music. Everyone in his family played a musical instrument. When he was four years old, Yo-Yo began taking **cello** (CHEL-oh) lessons. When he was five, he **memorized** (MEM-or-yzd) music by the famous composer Johannes Sebastian Bach. By the time he was nine, Yo-Yo Ma was famous. He had performed at Carnegie Hall in New York City. Today, Yo-Yo Ma is one of the greatest cello players of all time.

◀ Yo-Yo Ma has played with musicians from around the world.

13

Tiananmen Square

In 1989, about 100,000 students and workers in Beijing **demonstrated** (DEM-un-stray-ted) at a place called Tiananmen Square. They wanted to show the government that they disagreed with the way their country was ruled. The government did not like this and sent the Chinese army to stop the **protestors** (PRO-tes-terz). The situation became violent. About 5,000 people were killed, and 10,000 were hurt. It was a sad time for my parents and for many Chinese Americans.

What happened in Tiananmen Square in 1989 ▶
is an important part of Chinese history.

Clothing

In the past, Chinese people wore clothing that showed their **status** (STA-tus) in society. Working people wore pants and short jackets. Women who did not work wore a *cheongsam* (CHONG-sam), or a long dress.

Today, Chinese Americans follow their own styles of clothing. I like to wear T-shirts and jeans. Sometimes I wear a skirt or a dress. On special days, such as weddings or birthdays, we might wear the same kinds of clothes as our **ancestors** (AN-ses-terz).

◀ This woman is wearing traditional clothing from the Chinese province of Yunnan.

Chinese Food

My family likes to make dinner together. My mom or dad cuts meat, chicken, or fish into small pieces. Then we add them to vegetables. All of this is steamed or **stir-fried** (STER-fryd) with different spices in a large pot called a wok. We eat the food out of bowls with **chopsticks** (CHOP-stiks). We eat rice and drink tea with every meal.

On special occasions, my mom makes *jiao tse* (JOW-dze), or dumplings. *Jiao tse* is my favorite Chinese dish!

Chinese food has many different ▶ tastes and textures.

Tea

The Chinese were the first people to drink tea. We drink tea at every meal, but we don't put milk or sugar in it like some people do. There are two kinds of tea that my family likes to drink. Green tea is made from tea leaves that are slightly **fermented** (fer-MEN-ted). It has a strong flavor. Black tea is made from leaves that are completely fermented. It tastes bitter. My older brother likes to drink black tea, but I don't like it very much.

◀ Chinese people drink tea from small cups without handles.

21

I Am Chinese American

I have learned a lot from my parents about Chinese culture. They have told me that China is over 3,500 years old! It has many different **traditions** (truh-DISH-unz). My family celebrates some of them, such as the Chinese New Year. But we also like to follow American customs too, such as watching fireworks on the Fourth of July. I am happy to be living in America. But I am also proud of my Chinese **heritage** (HEHR-ih-tij).

Glossary

ancestor (AN-ses-ter) A person in your family who lived before you.

Beijing (bay-ZHING) The capital of China.

cello (CHEL-oh) A large stringed musical instrument.

cheongsam (CHONG-sam) A long dress with a high collar.

chopsticks (CHOP-stiks) Two very thin sticks used for eating.

Confucius (kun-FYOO-shus) A wise man and teacher who lived around 500 B.C.

culture (KUL-cher) The beliefs, customs, and religions of a group of people.

demonstrate (DEM-un-strayt) To gather together with other people to show how you feel about something.

ferment (fer-MENT) A chemical change in which the makeup of something changes.

heritage (HEHR-ih-tij) Cultural traditions that are handed down from parent to child.

jiao tse (JOW-dze) Chinese dumplings.

memorize (MEM-or-yz) To learn something and be able to repeat it.

protestor (PRO-tes-ter) A person who shows that he or she disagrees.

sage (SAYJ) A very wise person.

status (STA-tus) A person's position or rank.

stir-fry (STER-fry) To cook food in a pan with oil while stirring.

tradition (truh-DISH-un) The customs and beliefs that are handed down from parent to child.

23

Index